HOW TO GROW MARIJUANA LIGHTS

CANNABIS BOOK

By David Right

PREFACE

Cannabis, also known as marijuana or ganja, is a psychoactive product of the plant Cannabis sativa. The drug is commonly ingested after it is dried. The most common parts of the plants used in ingestion are dried flowers and leaves of the female plants. Another method of consumption is the resinous form, which consists of the crystalline trichomes on the flowers and leaves.

THC, or tetrahydrocannabinol, is the chemical responsible for most of marijuana's psychological effects. It acts much like the cannabinoid chemicals made naturally by the body, according to the National Institute on Drug Abuse (NIDA).

.

THC is one of many compounds found in the resin secreted by glands of the marijuana plant. More of these glands are found around the reproductive organs of the plant than on any other area of the plant. Other compounds uni☐ue to marijuana, called cannabinoids, are present in this resin. One cannabinoid, CBD is nonpsychoactive, according to the National Center for Biotechnology Information, and actually blocks the high associated with THC.

Contents

CHAPTER 1- WHAT IS MARIJUANA

Cannabis has connection with mankind for thousands of years. Cannabis has psychoactive and therapeutic qualities. The cannabis plant can grow up to five meters in height in the wild. It flowers between the fag end of the summer season to late autumn. The earliest reference to cannabis has been some Chinese records written in 2800 BC. Cannabis is a wild plant in many Asian countries. Cannabis is widely deemed to have originated in India. Many indigenous communities across the world have been using cannabis for several purposes like religious, recreational, and medical.

Many physicians prescribe medications having cannabis to patients suffering from such ailments as glaucoma, multiple sclerosis, HIV, and cancer, besides several others. Cannabis also provides the vim to the heart and the results have been proved to be akin to a person exercising regularly in the gymnasium!

Nowadays, cannabis is identified as a drug. Cannabis is banned in many countries. Often, cannabis users deprived of the drug have been found to be aggressive in nature. In other words, cannabis is addictive psychologically. The effect is quite similar to steroids that are anabolic in nature. What is more, addicts of several hard drugs have been found to be the sources of major sociological or health problems. But a study has shown that cannabis users are less prone to create such nuisances. More than 400 chemicals constitute cannabis. Cannabis has been used by many indigenous people because of its psychoactive effects. The primary psychoactive element in cannabis is 'THC' or tetrahydrocannabinol.

The cannabis plant, Cannabis sativa or Cannabis indica, is also known as hemp, cannabis, and marijuana. Cannabis is nicknamed variously as grass, resin, dope, herb, pot, smoke, puff, weed, marijuana, and ganja, besides the hundreds of other names. Despite the bans, many youth have been found to be hooked to cannabis across the globe.

The strongest and concentrated form of cannabis oil is manufactured from the cannabis resin. The resin is dissolved, filtered and finally evaporated. In the United Kingdom, this oil is bracketed along with cocaine and heroin and is a drug under the Class A classification.

The cannabis resin is extracted from the cannabis buds as blocks. These cannabis blocks are then heated and crumbled when they become ready for use.

The hue of the cannabis resin can vary from green to dark brown. This form is popularly called 'hash', 'soapbar' or 'black'.

The herbal form of cannabis is known as 'skunk', 'weed' or simply 'grass'. It is prepared from the dried or powdered buds of the cannabis plant.

Researches on cannabis have thrown up interesting data. Take for instance the finding approximately 46 per cent of people in the age group from 14 to 30 have been hooked to cannabis even if temporarily. What is more, 50 per cent of these people have subse□uently returned to the herb. Cannabis smoking has been found to be more popular then net surfing in the USA. While in the UK, as much as 78 per cent of the people held for drug related offenses have been found to possessing cannabis.

Physical and pharmacological effects of marijuana

Cannabis is not only the most abused illicit drug in the United States. it is in fact the most abused illegal drug worldwide (UNODC, 2010). In the United States, it is a schedule-I substance which means that it is legally considered as having no medical use and it is highly addictive (US DEA, 2010). Doweiko (2009) explains that not all cannabis has abuse potential. He, therefore, suggests using the common terminology marijuana when referring to cannabis with abuse potential. For the sake of clarity this terminology is used in this book as well.

Today, marijuana is at the forefront of international controversy debating the appropriateness of its widespread illegal status. In many Union states, it has become legalized for medical purposes. This trend is known as "medical marijuana" and is strongly applauded by advocates while simultaneously loathed harshly by opponents. It is in this context that it was decided to choose the topic of the physical and pharmacological effects of marijuana for the basis of this book research.

Marijuana is a plant more correctly called cannabis sativa. As mentioned, some cannabis sativa plants do not have abuse potential and are called hemp. Hemp is used widely for various fiber products including newspaper and artist's canvas. Cannabis sativa with abuse potential is what we call marijuana. It is interesting to note that although widely studies for many years, there is alot that researchers still do not know about marijuana. Neuroscientists and biologists know what the effects of marijuana are but they still do not fully understand why.

Deweiko (2009), Gold, Frost-Pineda, & Jacobs (2004) point out that of approximately four hundred known chemicals found in the cannabis plants, researchers know of over sixty that are thought to have psychoactive effects on the human brain. The most well known and potent of this is â-9-tetrahydrocannabinol, or THC. Like Hazelden (2005), Deweiko states that while we know many of the neurophysical effects of THC, the reasons THC produces these effects are unclear.

Neurobiology:

As a psychoactive substance, THC directly affects the central nervous system (CNS). It affects a massive range of neurotransmitters and catalyzes other biochemical and enzymatic activity as well. The CNS is stimulated when the THC activates specific neuroreceptors in the brain causing the various physical and emotional reactions that will be expounded on more specifically further on. The only substances that can activate neurotransmitters are substances that mimic chemicals that the brain produces naturally. The fact that THC stimulates brain function teaches scientists that the brain has natural cannabinoid receptors. It is still unclear why humans have natural cannabinoid receptors and how they work. What we do know is that marijuana will stimulate cannabinoid receptors up to twenty times more actively than any of the body's natural neurotransmitters ever could (Doweiko, 2009).

Perhaps the biggest mystery of all is the relationship between THC and the neurotransmitter serotonin. Serotonin receptors are among the most stimulated by all psychoactive drugs, but most specifically alcohol and nicotine. Independent of marijuana's relationship with the chemical, serotonin is already a little understood neurochemical and its supposed neuroscientific roles of functioning and purpose are still mostly hypothetical (Schuckit & Tapert, 2004). What neuroscientists have found definitively is that marijuana smokers have very high levels of serotonin activity (Hazelden, 2005). I would hypothesize that it may be this relationship between THC and serotonin that explains the "marijuana maintenance program" of achieving abstinence from alcohol and allows marijuana smokers to avoid painful withdrawal symptoms and avoid cravings from alcohol. The efficacy of "marijuana maintenance" for aiding alcohol abstinence is not scientific but is a phenomenon I have personally witnessed with numerous clients.

Interestingly, marijuana mimics so many neurological reactions of other drugs that it is extremely difficult to classify in a specific class. Researchers will place it in any of these categories: psychedelic; hallucinogen; or serotonin inhibitor. It has properties that mimic similar chemical responses as opioids. Other chemical responses mimic stimulants (Ashton, 2001; Gold, Frost-Pineda, & Jacobs, 2004). Hazelden (2005) classifies marijuana in its own special class - cannabinoids. The reason for this confusion is the complexity of the numerous psychoactive properties found within marijuana, both known and unknown. One recent client I saw could not recover from the visual distortions he suffered as a result of pervasive psychedelic use as long as he was still smoking marijuana. This seemed to be as a result of the psychedelic properties found within active cannabis (Ashton, 2001). Although not strong enough to produce these visual distortions on its own, marijuana was strong enough to prevent the brain from healing and recovering.

Emotions:

Cannibinoid receptors are located throughout the brain thus affecting a wide variety of functioning. The most important on the emotional level is the stimulation of the brain's nucleus accumbents perverting the brain's natural reward centers. Another is that of the amygdala which controls one's emotions and fears.

I have observed that the heavy marijuana smokers who I work with personally seem to share a commonality of using the drug to manage their anger. This observation has evidenced based consequences and is the basis of much scientific research. Research has in fact found that the relationship between marijuana and managing anger is clinically significant. Anger is a defense mechanism used to guard against emotional conse□uences of adversity fueled by fear. As stated, fear is a primary function controlled by the amygdala which is heavily stimulated by marijuana use.

Neurophysical Effects of THC:

Neurological messages between transmitters and receptors not only control emotions and psychological functioning. It is also how the body controls both volitional and nonvolitional functioning. The cerebellum and the basal ganglia control all bodily movement and coordination. These are two of the most abundantly stimulated areas of the brain that are triggered by marijuana. This explains marijuana's physiological effect causing altered blood pressure, and a weakening of the muscles (Doweiko, 2009). THC ultimately affects all neuromotor activity to some degree (Gold, Frost-Pineda, & Jacobs, 2004).

An interesting phenomena I have witnessed in almost all clients who identify marijuana as their drug of choice is the use of marijuana smoking before eating. This is explained by effects of marijuana on the "CB-1" receptor. The CB-1 receptors in the brain are found heavily in the limbic system, or the nucleolus accumbents, which controls the reward pathways. These reward pathways are what affect the appetite and eating habits as part of the body's natural survival instinct, causing us to crave eating food and rewarding us with dopamine when we finally do. Martin (2004) makes this connection, pointing out that uni☐ue to marijuana users is the stimulation of the CB-1 receptor directly triggering the appetite.

What is high grade and low grade?

A current client of mine explains how he originally smoked up to fifteen joints of "low grade" marijuana daily but eventually switched to "high grade" when the low grade was starting to prove ineffective. In the end, fifteen joints of high-grade marijuana were becoming ineffective for him as well. He often failed to get his "high" from that either. This entire process occurred within five years of the client's first ever experience with marijuana. What is high and low grade marijuana, and why would marijuana begin to lose its effects after a while?

The potency of marijuana is measured by the THC content within. As the market on the street becomes more competitive, the potency on the street becomes more pure. This has caused a trend in ever rising potency that responds to demand. One average joint of marijuana smoked today has the equivalent THC potency as ten average joints of marijuana smoked during the 1960's (Hazelden, 2005).

THC levels will depend mainly on what part of the cannabis leaf is being used for production. For instance cannabis buds can be between two to nine times more potent than fully developed leaves. Hash oil, a form of marijuana developed by distilling cannabis resin, can yield higher levels of THC than even high-grade buds (Gold, Frost-Pineda, & Jacobs, 2004).

Tolerance:

The need to raise the amount of marijuana one smokes, or the need to intensify from low grade to high grade is known clinically as tolerance. The brain is efficient. As it recognizes that neuroreceptors are being stimulated without the neurotransmitters emitting those chemical signals, the brain resourcefully lowers its chemical output so the total levels are back to normal. The smoker will not feel the high anymore as his brain is now "tolerating" the higher levels of chemicals and he or she is back to feeling normal. The smoker now raises the dose to get the old high back and the cycle continues. The smoker may find switching up in grades effective for a while. Eventually, the brain can cease to produce the chemical altogether, entirely relying on the synthetic version being ingested (Gold, Frost-Pineda, & Jacobs, 2004; Hazelden, 2005).

Why isn't there any withdrawal?

The flip side of the tolerance process is known as "dependence." As the body stops producing its own natural chemicals, it now needs the marijuana user to continue smoking in order to continue the functioning of chemicals without interruption. The body is now ordering the ingestion of the THC making it extremely difficult to quit. In fact, studies show that marijuana dependency is even more powerful than seemingly harder drugs like cocaine (Gold, Frost-Pineda, & Jacobs, 2004).

With ☐uitting other drugs like stimulants, opioids, or alcohol the body reacts in negative and sometimes severely dangerous ways. This is due to the sudden lack of chemical input tied together with the fact that the brain has stopped its own natural neurotransmission of those chemicals long ago. This is the phenomenon of withdrawal (Haney, 2004; Hazelden, 2005; Jaffe & Jaffe, 2004; Tabakoff & Hoffman, 2004).

While research has shown comparable withdrawal reactions is marijuana users as in alcohol or other drugs (Ashton, 2001), what I have witnessed many times in my personal interaction with clients is the apparent lack of withdrawal experienced by most marijuana users. Of course they experience cravings, but they don't report having the same neurophysical withdrawal reaction that the other drug users have. Some marijuana smokers use this as their final proof that marijuana "is not a drug" and they should, therefore, not be subjugated to the same treatment and pursuit of recovery efforts as other drug or alcohol abusers.

The reality is that the seemingly lack of acute withdrawal is a product of the uniqueness of how the body stores THC. While alcohol and other drugs are out of a persons system within a one to five days (Schuckit & Tapert, 2004), THC can take up to thirty days until it is fully expelled from the body (Doweiko, 2009). When THC is ingested by the smoker, it is initially distributed very rapidly through the heart, lungs, and brain (Ashton, 2001). THC however, is eventually converted into protein and becomes stored is body fat and muscle. This second process of storage in body fat reserve is a far slower process. When the user begins abstinence, fat stored THC begins its slow release back into the blood stream. While the rate of reentry into the body's system is too slow to produce any psychoactive effects, it will aid in easing the former smoker through the withdrawal process in a more manageable and pain free manner. The more one smokes the more one stores. The more body mass the smoker has, the more THC can be stored up as well (Doweiko, 2009). Thus, in very large clients seen, it take up to thirty days before urine screens show a cleared THC level.

Similar to THC's slow taper like cleansing is the slow rate of initial onset of psychoactive response. Clients report that they do not get high smoking marijuana right away - it takes them time for their bodies to get used to it before they feel high. This is explained by the slow absorption of THC into fatty tissue reaching peak concentrations in 4-5 days. As the THC begins to release slowly into the blood stream, the physiological response will become heightened rapidly with every new smoking of marijuana resulting in another high. As the user repeats this process and high levels of THC accumulate in the body and continue to reach the brain, the THC is finally distributed to the neocortical, limbic, sensory, and motor areas that were detailed earlier (Ashton, 2001).

Physiology:

The neurology and neurophysiology of marijuana has been described thus far. There are many physical components of marijuana smoking as well. National Institute on Drug Abuse (2010) reports that marijuana smokers can have many of the same respiratory problems as tobacco smokers including daily cough, phlegm production, more fre□uent acute chest illness, and a heightened risk of lung infections. They quote research showing evidence that chronic marijuana smokers, who do not smoke tobacco, have more health problems than non- smokers because of respiratory illnesses.

The definitive research documenting the significant negative biophysical health effects of marijuana is not conclusive. We do know that marijuana smoke contains fifty to seventy percent more carcinogenic hydrocarbons than tobacco smoke does (Ashton, 2001; Gold, Frost-Pineda, & Jacobs, 2004; NIDA, 2010). While some research shows that marijuana smokers show dysregulated growth of epithelial cells in their lung tissue which can lead to cancer, other studies have shown no positive associations at all between marijuana use and lung, upper respiratory, or upper digestive tract cancers (NIDA, 2010). Perhaps the most eye opening fact of all is that all experts agree that historically there has yet to be a single documented death reported purely as a result of marijuana smoking (Doweiko, 2009; Gold, Frost-Pineda, & Jacobs, 2004; Nakaya, 2007; Van Tuyl, 2007).

Pharmacology - "Medical Marijuana":

This last fact regarding the seemingly less harmful effects of marijuana smoking even in comparison with legal drugs like alcohol and nicotine is most often the very first ⬜uoted by proponents of legalizing marijuana for its positive medical advantages. Nakaya (2007) points to the seemingly positive effects of marijuana on alzheimers, cancer, multiple sclerosis, glaucoma, and AIDS. While not scientific, personal experiences of the positive relief of sufferers from chronic illness is ⬜uoted as benefits that are claimed to outweigh the negative effects.

Van Tuyl (2007) states "almost all drugs - including those that are legal - pose greater threats to individual health and/or society than does marijuana." She agrees that legalizing the smoking of marijuana would not justify the positive effects but posits still that the risks associated with smoking can be "mitigated by alternate routes of administration, such as vaporization". The arguments point to clinically riskier drugs like opioids, benzodiazepines, and amphetamines that are administered by prescription on a daily basis. These drugs, like Vicodin, Xanex, or Ritalin, are internationally acceptable when deemed "medically necessary."

17

Conclusion / Reflection:

While I am not comfortable weighing in on the controversy of the legalization of marijuana, in conclusion of this research paper there are clear implications for me as a practitioner. Alcohol too is quite legal, as is nicotine, but for the addiction counselor, it is important to continue keeping a directive on the biopsychosocial considerations regarding the misuse of any substance. Because of the large lack of empirical knowledge regarding the neurobiological properties associated with exact brain functioning, a crucial focus moving forward will prove to be keeping tabs on breakthrough discoveries in the neuroscience of THC and other cannabinoids. The discoveries of particular importance for current practice are the pathology of marijuana's relationship with emotional self-medication, tolerance, and most of all the withdrawal process. I have already begun to utilize the knowledge of the physical and pharmacological effects of marijuana expressed heretofore with personal success and look forward to continue utilizing farther research to do the same.

CHAPTER 2- HOW TO USE MARIJUANA

Yet, somehow, this fact fails to hold true for weed smokers. Is this a natural anomaly? Well, kind of. Recent studies show that regular cannabis users are as likely to get lung cancer as the average person.

Weird, right? How is that possible? Well, we've got the scoop. Here's all you've ever needed to know about the effects of smoking marijuana, and how to keep your lungs healthy while doing it:

Earlier this year, researchers at Atlanta's Emory University analyzed data from the National Health and Nutrition Examination Survey. Their study found that marijuana users who smoked one joint a day for up to 20 years did not show signs of lung damage.

These results were found by studying data from a type of breathing test that measures airflow as you exhale. This test is called a spirometry test in the medical world.

But, wait! There's more.

A 2014 and a 2006 study both found that smoking cannabis DID leave tar behind in our lungs. BUT, somehow, lung cancer risk remains relatively low despite that fact.

Bad News For Heavy Smokers

Lung respiratory

Studies shows a slice of lung tissue with inflammation and irritation of the airways in the lungs caused by smoking.

While cannabis and lung cancer don't go hand-in-hand, heavy smokers still have some risks to worry about:

Trouble Exhaling

Heavy smokers that crossed the joint-a-day for over 20 years threshold lost some of their capacity to make full, forced exhalations.

Inflammation: Long-term, heavy smokers also had more inflammation in the small air pathways in the lungs. This can cause asthma-like symptoms later in life.

These risks are reduced when you vaporize instead of smoke herb. While it may seem obvious, it's easy to forget that when you smoke weed, you're breathing hot, smoldering plant materials into your body. Vapes use just enough heat to activate the cannabinoids in your flower or wax. At the same time, they avoid the itchy, inflaming burn associated with weed that's been roasted a little too hot.

Rolling papers and the products you use to smoke may also be to blame for some of the lung irritation. Rolling papers may be processed with bleach or other chemicals, damaging your lung tissue. Switching to a vape would avoid all of these risks as well.

But… Why Don't Weed Smokers Get Lung Cancer?

Doctors, researchers, and scientists are still puzzled about why marijuana smoke is not linked to cancer. It's been recorded for some time now that marijuana smoke contains many of the same cancer-causing toxins as tobacco.

The odd absence of tumors might be explained by THC, the primary psychoactive in weed. Research coming out of Spain's oldest university, the Complutense University of Madrid, has shown that THC causes tumor cells to destroy themselves in animals.

No official studies have yet been approved to test THC's power as a true tumor-killer in humans. Though, fortunately, there's hope in animal testing. In animal models, THC both slowed and helped prevent the growth and progression of tumor growth.

Another study from a German University tested the effects of cannabidiol CBD on lung cancer cells. The results were quite exciting: CBD may help prevent cancers from moving around the body. That is to say, it prevents cancer cells from infecting other cells.

The authors even went as far as suggesting clinical trials using CBD as a treatment for lung cancer.

Findings like this may point to why weed smoke doesn't cause lung cancer. Can a substance cause cancer and also prevent it at the same time? Only time and research will tell.

Different Smokes for Different Folks

Everyone has their preferred method of smoking weed. Joints, pipes, and blunts have always been crowd pleasers. However, now that concentrates are in the mix, there's a little more you need to know if you want to be a health-conscious cannabis smoker.

Protecting your lungs starts with knowing the pros and cons of different smoking methods.

Vaporization

Using a vape is the healthiest way of consuming cannabis by smoking. Because vaporizers don't put direct fire onto the herb, you're able to get a nice inhale of vapors while mitigating many of the harmful impacts of inhaling hot plant material.

Joints & Pipes

There's one thing you need to remember before you light up: your standard Bic Lighter can reach a temperature of 3,590.6 degrees F (1,977 C). That. Is. Hot. Smoking a joint, pre-roll, or a pipe means taking a very hot flame directly to your weed. You inhale the remaining hot, ashey particles in less than a second after lighting the herb.

That hot, unfiltered smoke is what causes irritation and tar build-up. Looking to play it safe? Try natural rolling papers or consider a screen for your pipe.

Water Pipes & Bongs

Water pipes, bubblers, and bongs all use water to cool down smoke before you breathe it into your throat and lungs. Not only does this cool down your herb, but the water also catches unnecessary ash and weed particles that would later turn into tar inside your lungs.

These water-based methods are far from perfect. Water and ice don't catch all of the plant resin floating around in smoke. Look for larger pieces that increase the distance between the flame and you, and supplement with ice if you'd like to play it safe.

Dabbing

Dabbing concentrates like Butane Hash Oil (BHO) is now more popular than ever. For healthy lungs, there are a couple of important things to note about dabbing:

Use Ice: Using a torch makes the smoke much, much hotter than any other method. Cool things down by using a water-based rig and crushed ice.

Solvents Matter: The health risks of inhaling small amounts of butane are controversial. For the most part, butane burns hot and evaporates fast. Much of it is gone the moment the torch hits the wax. However, too much gas can cause headaches and irritate mucous membranes as you inhale. If you find BHO a little uncomfortable, CO_2 extractions are easier on the lungs.

OK, here it is: the final tip on how to keep your lungs healthy while smoking weed. When you can, just say no to schwag. "Schwag" meaning flower or wax that just doesn't look or taste □uite right. We're talking sketchy, real low-□uality stuff. Here's why:

The Bad News:

Unfortunately, at the time of writing, there is no standardized □uality control for marijuana. Without testing data, there's no way to tell if what you're smoking is free of contaminants. Those contaminants may be leftover pesticide, fertilizer, miticide, fungus, or something else that happened to hitch a ride on what you just picked up.

Like inhaling too much butane solvent, breathing in unknown substances has consequences. Smoking pollutants can cause coughing, lung and throat irritation, and allergic reactions.

The Good News:

Many legal states now mandate that grown cannabis legally is tracked and tested. People are demanding better □uality marijuana, and their voices are being heard.

More and more, growers and dispensary owners are having products tested. This ensures that the plants are healthy and safe for consumption. This testing data is available online. If you're lucky enough to live with access to legal medical or recreational cannabis, ask your dispensary for local testing data.

Cleaning Your Lungs After Smoking

You might be wondering: If smoking leaves all this extra stuff behind, is there a way to clean out my lungs?

The answer? Yes! A little exercise can help reduce the effects of marijuana on your lungs. The best exercise for your lungs? Deep breathing.

Why Breath Matters

As we breathe, we take in vital oxygen that keeps us alive. There are two primary types of breathing: deep breathing and shallow breathing.

As we inhale, we either take air into the tops of our lungs, or we breathe deeply and fully throughout the organs. The more fully we breathe, the more fresh oxygen can travel deeply into the lung tissue. The shallower the breath, the more toxins, stale air, pollutants, and allergens stay trapped.

All this trapped bad air and extra gunk in our lungs has direct impacts on our health. It causes us to feel tired and leads to a loss of tissue function.

Lazy Lungs

Lungs need exercise and movement every single day. When we're sitting and resting, our lungs only operate at 50% capacity.

"Your lungs need at the very least 20 minutes of consistent, moderately intense movement daily, like a brisk walk," explains Jennifer Ryan, PT. Jennifer is a specialist in cardiovascular and pulmonary physical therapy at Rush University Medical Center.

"To help counteract the build-up of toxins and tar in the lungs caused by environmental pollutants," Ryan continues, "allergens, dust, and cigarette some, you need to help your lungs cleanse themselves."

Care about your lungs? Set aside time for few simple breathing exercises after your next bowl. They will give your lungs the fresh oxygen and exercise they need to feel healthy. To get you started, we've outlined few of our favorites.

Breathing Exercises to Clear Out the Smoke

These □uick and simple breathing exercises eliminate toxins and keep airways clear. As an added bonus, they may even help you de-stress.

For all of these exercises, it's important to think about your posture. Slouching or hunching hinders your ability to breath deeply. If you're seated, plant your feet flat on the floor. Remember to keep your back straight and your chest open.

If you chose to lay down, lay flat on your back with your arms relaxed down from your sides. Keep your palms open.

Breathing

Inhale for 4 seconds, hold for 7, and exhale for 8. The 4-7-8 technique has grown in popularity among insomniacs and anxiety sufferers alike. Not only will each breath help clear out your lungs, but it will leave you feeling calm and relaxed.

Deep Belly Breath Breathing

Focus on long, slow inhalations and exhalations of five seconds or longer. Imagine that you are breathing deep into your belly. Concentrate on raising your chest and navel as you inhale.

The Cleansing Breath Pranayama

The strength of this breath comes from the abdominal muscles. Stand with your feet hip-width apart. This breath should not be done lying down. Exhale using short contractions of your abdominal muscles for power. Remember to keep your mouth relaxed open.

Diaphragmatic Breathing

Visualize expanding the diaphragm as you slowly and deeply inhale. The diaphragm is a muscle at the base of your lungs. Singers exercise this muscle to increase their lung capacity.

Lung Cleansing Herbs for Your Vape

Marijuana might be our favorite herb, but many other plants also have powerful medicinal properties.

Cultures have been using medicinal herbs to treat respiratory illnesses for centuries. As early as the fifth century B.C., common plants like celery were used as medicines.

Celery, often found lying limp and pathetic in the bottom of the salad crisper, is antispasmodic. In ancient England and China, it was used to treat diseases like asthma and bronchitis. Other medicinal plants can:

Break up mucus and expel congestion.

Calm inflammatory and allergic reactions.

Reduce cell damage and redness as antioxidants.

Ease coughing symptoms.

Kill harmful organisms and bacteria.

To help refresh your lungs after smoking weed, sprinkle a little of the dried herbs listed below into a vape. You can also brew them into a nice cup of tea.

Other ways of using marijuana

Not everyone likes to smoke, and those with compromised lung health may not even have the option. The stigmatized image of smoking might be the only thing stopping some people from trying cannabis, even if they live in a state with legal marijuana (maybe you can see your mom taking a bong rip, but I sure can't).

Even though there are a number of different ways you can consume cannabis that have evolved over the years, you may be looking for a more health-conscious option. Here are some suggestions for a smoke-free cannabis experience.

1. Vaporizing

Vaporizing cannabis

You don't need to torch your cannabis with a lighter to reap its benefits; actually, its chemical compounds vaporize at a much lower, less harmful temperature. The taste of vaporized cannabis is often preferred to that of combusted flower, and the vapor is much easier on the lungs. Larger table-top vaporizers can offer high-□uality vapor with advanced temperature settings, while small hand-held devices let you enjoy cannabis flower or oils wherever you go. These days there are many affordable vaporizers to choose from if you're interested in trying out this smokeless form of cannabis consumption.

2. Edibles

cannabis-infused edibles

One of the more obvious alternatives to smoking is cannabis-infused food and drink. The diversity of marijuana edibles is quickly and vastly expanding, so much so that you can infuse virtually anything that calls for butter or oil. You can make your own at home (it's surprisingly easy, but be cautious with dosing), but dispensaries and retail shops often have a staggering number of options, from infused lemonade to roasted garlic crackers. You've probably heard it already, but it must be said: start with a low dose and be patient. Because of the digestive process, edibles take much longer to kick in and can have intensely psychoactive effects.

3. Ingestible Oils

cannabis oil

Ingestible oils are basically any cannabis concentrate that is taken orally. These most commonly come in capsules or plastic applicators, either of which can be consumed directly or added to food or drink. Like edibles, ingestible oils can induce powerful effects that take a while to kick in, so be mindful of your dose!

4. Tinctures

cannabis tinctures

Tinctures are infused liⵏuids that extract cannabis compounds using an alcohol soak and are applied directly under the tongue. Unlike ingestible oils and infused foods, tinctures enter the bloodstream immediately, allowing for fast-acting effects and better dose control. A variety of flavors, potencies, and cannabinoid profiles are often available, catering to your specific preferences or medical needs.

5. Topicals

cannabis topicals

Topicals are cannabis-infused lotions and balms that are applied directly to the skin for localized relief of pain, soreness, and inflammation. One uni☐ue property of cannabis topicals is their ability to treat symptoms without psychoactive effects, so if you need to be clear-headed and bypass that euphoric high altogether, topicals are the way to go.

6. Dabbing

dabbing

Dabbing is a method of flash-vaporization in which cannabis concentrates are dropped on a heated water-pipe attachment and inhaled for intensely potent effects. The attachment is a glass or metallic nail that's heated up using a butane torch – and if that sounds sketchy to you, the public eye would not disagree. But dabbing enthusiasts typically elect this method because (a) properly refined concentrates offer a clean experience free of plant material, and (b) dabbing produces a vapor as opposed to smoke. It may not be the option you suggest to a first-time cannabis consumer, but it's certainly an option for graduates.

CHAPTER 3- ADVANTAGES OF MARIJUANA CANNABIS

States around the country — more than 20 in total — have legalized medical marijuana.

Experts have been changing their minds too — recently, CNN's chief medical correspondent Sanjay Gupta reversed his opinion on medical marijuana.

While recreational pot usage is controversial, many people agree with Gupta's new stance, and believe that the drug should be legal for medical uses.

And even though the benefits of smoking pot may be overstated by advocates of marijuana legalization, new laws will help researchers study the drug's medicinal uses and better understand how it impacts the body.

Currently only 6% of studies on marijuana analyze its medicinal properties.

Keep in mind, though, that there are negative effects of smoking too much pot or using it for non-medicinal purposes. When overused or abused, pot can lead to dependency and mess with your memory and emotions.

There are at least two active chemicals in marijuana that researchers think have medicinal applications. Those are cannabidiol (CBD) — which seems to impact the brain without a high— and tetrahydrocannabinol (THC) — which has pain relieving (and other) properties.

Also keep in mind that some of these health benefits can potentially be gained by taking THC pills like Dronabinol, a synthetic form of THC, which in some ways might be more effective than smoked marijuana.

Randy Astaiza contributed to an earlier version of this story.

It can be used to treat Glaucoma.

Marijuana use can be used to treat and prevent the eye disease glaucoma, which increases pressure in the eyeball, damaging the optic nerve and causing loss of vision.

Marijuana decreases the pressure inside the eye, according to the National Eye Institute: "Studies in the early 1970s showed that marijuana, when smoked, lowered intraocular pressure (IOP) in people with normal pressure and those with glaucoma."

These effects of the drug may slow the progression of the disease, preventing blindness.

It may help reverse the carcinogenic effects of tobacco and improve lung health.

According to a study published in Journal of the American Medical Association in January 2012, marijuana does not impair lung function and can even increase lung capacity.

Researchers looking for risk factors of heart disease tested the lung function of 5,115 young adults over the course of 20 years. Tobacco smokers lost lung function over time, but pot users actually showed an increase in lung capacity.

It's possible that the increased lung capacity maybe due to taking a deep breath while inhaling the drug and not from a therapeutic chemical in the drug.

It can help control epileptic seizures.

Marijuana use can prevent epileptic seizures, a 2003 study showed.

Robert J. DeLorenzo, of Virginia Commonwealth University, gave marijuana extract and synthetic marijuana to epileptic rats. The drugs rid the rats of the seizures for about 10 hours. Cannabinoids like the active ingredients in marijuana, tetrahydrocannabinol (also known as THC), control seizures by binding to the brain cells responsible for controlling excitability and regulating relaxation.

The findings were published in the Journal of Pharmacology and Experimental Therapeutics.

It also decreases the symptoms of a severe seizure disorder known as Dravet's Syndrome.

During the research for his documentary "Weed," Gupta interviewed the Figi family, who treats their 5-year-old daughter using a medical marijuana strain high in cannabidiol and low in THC.

Their daughter, Charlotte, has Dravet Syndrome, which causes seizures and severe developmental delays.

According to the film, the drug has decreased her seizures from 300 a week to just one every seven days. Forty other children in the state are using the same strain of marijuana to treat their seizures — and it seems to be working.

The doctors who recommended this treatment say that the cannabidiol in the plant interacts with the brain cells to quiet the excessive activity in the brain that causes these seizures.

As Gutpa notes, a Florida hospital that specializes in the disorder, the American Academy of Pediatrics, and the Drug Enforcement agency don't endorse marijuana as a treatment for Dravet or other seizure disorders.

A chemical found in marijuana stops cancer from spreading.

CBD may help prevent cancer from spreading, researchers at California Pacific Medical Center in San Francisco reported in 2007.

Cannabidiol stops cancer by turning off a gene called Id-1, the study, published in the journal Molecular Cancer Therapeutics, found. Cancer cells make more copies of this gene than non-cancerous cells, and it helps them spread through the body.

The researchers studied breast cancer cells in the lab that had high expression levels of Id-1 and treated them with cannabidiol. After treatment the cells had decreased Id-1 expression and were less aggressive spreaders.

In "WEED," Gupta also mentioned few studies in the U.S., Spain, and Israel that suggest the compounds in cannabis could even kill cancer cells.

It may decrease anxiety.

Medical marijuana users claim the drug helps relieve pain and suppress nausea — the two main reasons it's often used to relieve the side effects of chemotherapy.

In 2010, researchers at Harvard Medical School suggested that that some of the drug's benefits may actually be from reduced anxiety, which would improve the smoker's mood and act as a sedative in low doses.

Beware, though, higher doses may increase anxiety and make you paranoid.

THC slows the progression of Alzheimer's disease.

Marijuana may be able to slow the progression of Alzheimer's disease, a study led by Kim Janda of the Scripps Research Institute suggests.

The 2006 study, published in the journal Molecular Pharmaceutics, found that THC, the active chemical in marijuana, slows the formation of amyloid pla☐ues by blocking the enzyme in the brain that makes them. These pla☐ues are what kill brain cells and cause Alzheimer's.

The drug eases the pain of multiple sclerosis.

Marijuana may ease painful symptoms of multiple sclerosis, a study published in the Canadian Medical Association Journal in May suggests.
Jody Corey-Bloom studied 30 multiple sclerosis patients with painful contractions in their muscles. These patients didn't respond to other treatments, but after smoking marijuana for a few days they were in less pain.

The THC in the pot binds to receptors in the nerves and muscles to relieve pain. Other studies suggest that the chemical also helps control the muscle spasms.

Other types of muscle spasms could be helped too.

Other types of muscle spasms respond to marijuana as well. Gupta also found a teenager named Chaz who was using medical marijuana to treat diaphragm spasms that were untreatable by other, prescribed and very strong, medications.

His condition is called myoclonus diaphragmatic flutter (also known as Leeuwenhoek's Disease) and causes non -stop spasming in the abdominal muscles which are not only painful, but interfere with breathing and speaking.

Smoking marijuana is able to calm the attacks almost immediately, as it calms the muscles of the diaphragm.

It lessens side effects from treating hepatitis C and increases treatment effectiveness.

California dispensaries have been the subject of federal raidsReuters

Treatment for hepatitis C infection is harsh — negative side effects include fatigue, nausea, muscle aches, loss of appetite, and depression — and lasts for months. Many people aren't able to finish their treatment course because of the side effects.

But, pot to the rescue: A 2006 study in the European Journal of Gastroenterology and Hepatology found that 86% of patients using marijuana successfully completed their Hep C therapy, while only 29% of non-smokers completed their treatment, possibly because the marijuana helps lessens the treatments side effects.

Marijuana also seems to improve the treatment's effectiveness: 54% of hep C patients smoking marijuana got their viral levels low and kept them low, in comparison to only 8% of nonsmokers.

Marijuana treats inflammatory bowel diseases.

Patients with inflammatory bowel diseases like Crohn's disease and ulcerative colitis could benefit from marijuana use, studies suggest.

University of Nottingham researchers found in 2010 that chemicals in marijuana, including THC and cannabidiol, interact with cells in the body that play an important role in gut function and immune responses. The study was published in the Journal of Pharmacology and Experimental Therapeutics.

THC-like compounds made by the body increase the permeability of the intestines, allowing bacteria in. The plant-derived cannabinoids in marijuana block this body-cannabinoids, preventing this permeability and making the intestinal cells bond together tighter.

It relieves arthritis discomfort.

Marijuana alleviates pain reduces inflammation, and promotes sleep, which may help relieve pain and discomfort for people with rheumatoid arthritis, researchers announced in 2011.

Researchers from rheumatology units at several hospitals gave their patients Sativex, a cannabinoid-based pain-relieving medicine. After a two-week period, people on Sativex had a significant reduction in pain and improved sleep □uality compared to placebo users.

It keeps you skinny and helps your metabolism.

A study published in the American Journal Of Medicine on April 15 of last year suggested that pot smokers are skinnier than the average person and have healthier metabolism and reaction to sugars, even though they do end up eating more calories because of the munchies.

The study analyzed data from more than 4,500 adult Americans — 579 of whom were current marijuana smokers, meaning they had smoked in the last month. About 2,000 had used marijuana in the past, while another 2,000 had never used the drug.

They studied their body's response to eating sugars: their levels of the hormone insulin and their blood sugar levels while they had not eaten in nine hours, and after eating sugar.

Not only are pot users skinnier, but their body has a healthier response to sugar.

It improves the symptoms of Lupus, an autoimmune disorder.

Leonard C. Sperling, M.D., COL, MC, USA, Department of Dermatology, Uniformed Services University

Medical marijuana is being used to treat the autoimmune disease Systemic Lupus Erythematosus, which is when the body starts attacking itself for some unknown reason.

Some chemicals in marijuana seem to have a calming effect on the immune system, which may be how it helps deal with symptoms of Lupus. The rest of the positive impact of the marijuana is probably from the effects on pain and nausea.

While not really a health benefit, marijuana spurs creativity in the brain.

Contrary to stoner stereotypes, marijuana usage has actually been shown to have some positive mental effects, particularly in terms of increasing creativity. Even though people's short-term memories tend to function worse when high, people get better at tests requiring them to come up with new ideas.

One study tested participants on their ability to come up with different words related to a concept and found that using cannabis allowed people to come up with a greater range of related concepts, seeming "to make the brain better at detecting those remote associations that lead to radically new ideas," according to Wired.

Other researchers have found that some participants improve their "verbal fluency," their ability to come up with different words, while using marijuana.

Part of this increased creative ability may come from the release of dopamine in the brain, lessening inhibitions and allowing people to feel more relaxed, giving the brain the ability to perceive things differently.

Marijuana might be able to help with Crohn's disease.

Crohn's disease is an inflammatory bowel disorder that causes pain, vomiting, diarrhea, weight loss, and more. But a recent study in Israel showed that smoking a joint significantly reduced Crohn's disease symptoms in 10 out of 11 patients, and caused a complete remission of the disease in five of those patients.

That's a small study, but other research has shown similar effects. The cannabinoids from marijuana seem to help the gut regulate bacteria and intestinal function.

Pot soothes tremors for people with Parkinson's disease.

Recent research from Israel shows that smoking marijuana significantly reduces pain and tremors and improves sleep for Parkinson's disease patients. Particularly impressive was the improved fine motor skills among patients.

Medical marijuana is legal in Israel for multiple conditions, and alot of research into the medical uses of cannabis is done there, supported by the Israeli government.

Marijuana helps veterans suffering from PTSD.

The Department of Health and Human Services recently signed off on a proposal to study marijuana's potential as part of treatment for veterans with post-traumatic stress disorder.

Marijuana is approved to treat PTSD in some states already. In New Mexico, PTSD is the number one reason for people to get a license for medical marijuana, but this is the first time the U.S. government has approved a proposal that incorporates smoked or vaporized marijuana, which is currently classified by the government as a drug with no accepted medical applications.

Naturally occurring cannabinoids, similar to THC, help regulate the system that causes fear and anxiety in the body and brain.

Marijuana protects the brain after a stroke.

Research from the University of Nottingham shows that marijuana may help protect the brain from damage caused by stroke, by reducing the size of the area affected by the stroke — at least in rats, mice, and monkeys.

This isn't the only research that has shown neuroprotective effects from cannabis. Some research shows that the plant may help protect the brain after other traumatic events, like concussions.

It might protect the brain from concussions and trauma.

There is some evidence that marijuana can help heal the brain after a concussion or other traumatic injury. A recent study in the journal Cerebral Cortex showed that in mice, marijuana lessened the bruising of the brain and helped with healing mechanisms after a traumatic injury.

Harvard professor emeritus of psychiatry and marijuana advocate Lester Grinspoon recently wrote an open letter to NFL Commissioner Roger Goodell, saying the NFL should stop testing players for marijuana, and that the league should start funding research into the plant's ability to protect the brain.

"Already, many doctors and researchers believe that marijuana has incredibly powerful neuroprotective properties, an understanding based on both laboratory and clinical data," he writes.

Goodell recently said that he'd consider permitting athletes to use marijuana if medical research shows that it's an effective neuroprotective agent.

It can help eliminate nightmares.

This is a complicated one, because it involves effects that can be both positive and negative. Marijuana disturbs sleep cycles by interrupting the later stages of REM sleep. In the long run, this could be a problem for fre☐uent users.

However, for people suffering from serious nightmares, especially those associated with PTSD, this can be helpful. Nightmares and other dreams occur during those same stages of sleep. By interrupting REM sleep, many of those dreams may not occur. Research into using a synthetic cannabinoid, like THC, but not the same, showed a significant decrease in the number of nightmares in patients with PTSD.

Additionally, even if fre☐uent use can be bad for sleep, marijuana may be a better sleep aid than some other substances that people use. Some of those, including medication and alcohol, may potentially have even worse effects on sleep, though more research is needed on the topic.

Weed reduces some of the awful pain and nausea from chemo, and stimulates appetite.

One of the most well-known medical uses of marijuana is for people going through chemotherapy.

Cancer patients being treated with chemo suffer from painful nausea, vomiting, and loss of appetite. This can cause additional health complications.

Marijuana can help reduce these side effects, alleviating pain, decreasing nausea, and stimulating the appetite. There are also multiple FDA-approved cannabinoid drugs that use THC, the main active chemical in marijuana, for the same purposes.

Marijuana can help people trying to cut back on drinking.

Marijuana is safer than alcohol. That's not to say it's completely risk free, but it's much less addictive and doesn't cause nearly as much physical damage.

Disorders like alcoholism involve disruptions in the endocannabinoid system. Because of that, some people think cannabis might help patients struggling with those disorders.

Research in Harm Reduction Journal shows that some people use marijuana as a less harmful substitute for alcohol, prescription drugs, and other illegal drugs. Some of the most common reasons for patients to make that substitution are the less adverse side effects from marijuana and the fact that it is less likely to cause withdrawal problems.

Some people do become psychologically dependent on marijuana, and this doesn't mean that it's a cure for substance abuse problems. But, from a harm-reduction standpoint, it can help.

CHAPTER 4- GROWING MARIJUANA CANNABIS INDOOR

GROWING CANNABIS INDOORS

Choosing a variety is of major importance.

Yields and quality of plants grown under artificial lights mostly depend on:

1. the seed variety,

2. whether the plants are grown from seeds or clones,

3. after how many days of growing the plants are put into flowering, and

4. the optimization of the climatic conditions of the grow-room.

5. Indica or sativa content of the plant .

Apart from "true breeding" varieties, seeds collection consists of different F-1 hybrids. Crossing two "true breeding" strains (hybridizing) gives F-1 hybrids that possess the so-called "Hybrid Vigor". This means that the F-1 generation is a lot more potent than either parent. F-1 generations also consist of uniform plants.

Growing cannabis indoors has seen a dramatic rise in popularity in recent years. When done properly it produces excellent □uality stash which is usually much better than that sold on the streets. Growing cannabis indoors relies on the use of powerful artificial lights to replicate the effect of the sun. These lights typically take hundreds of Watts of electrical power to run and are commonly HPS (High Pressure Sodium) ut fluorescent lights, metal halide, LED light and other kinds have all been used successfully.

Cannabis loves light and the successful indoor grower tries to deliver as much light as possible. Consider 250 watts/m² only as a minimum starting point and realistically aim for 2-3 times that level if possible. More light will mean bigger, denser buds and superior yields. As well as delivering high light levels the successful indoor grower keeps the plants as near the light as possible to maximise the light intensity reaching the leaves and buds. Often the personal medical or recreational grower will have a growing area of 1-2 m² designed below a single 400W or 600W high-pressure sodium (HPS) lamp.

The indoor cannabis grower has to be careful that the plant doesn't grow too near to the hot light and damage itself. If the light feels cool to the back of the hand it will be cool for the plant also. For a 400W lamp, growers may not want to allow plants to grow within 40-50cm of the bulb. Cannabis plants can be bent over and tied if they get too tall, some indoor growers deliberately train their plants this way to get as much of the plant as possible close (but not too close) to the high intensity light.

Certain strains respond well to having the growing tip of the plant pinched out (known as 'topping', 'FIM' or pinching) after the 4th or 5th leaf pair. The resulting plants are often smaller and bushy without the dominant main growth stem (or 'cola') and are preferred for some smaller growrooms.

Some indoor growers train the plants underneath a metal chickenwire-style screen allowing only the buds to grow vertically while the stem and growing part of the plant grow horizontally. This SCROG (screen of green) techniᐤue allows the indoor grower to keep as much of the bud growth as possible equidistant to the lamp, maximising the efficiency and yield.

Specialist suppliers offer 'air cooled' lights for the indoor grower that enclose the light in a glass casing. A fan forces air over the light and outside the growroom via tubing, keeping the grow room cool and allowing the plants to grow taller without burning.Grow rooms are typically kept between 24°C -30°C for optimum results. Higher temperatures can cause the plants to wilt and cooler temperatures may slow down growth. The plants will need a gentle breeze from a fan, and a steady supply of fresh air which can be from your house or from outside. Stale air from the growroom is normally continually extracted outdoors by a fan and de-odorised with a carbon filter.

Those indoor growers that do get caught are often betrayed by the smell of their grow room, so some also invest in ozone generators to further remove odours from the exhausted grow room air.

Germinating cannabis seeds can be done in various ways and the internet is full of cannabis grow forums that document various methods. One simple method is to simply place seeds about 1cm below the surface of firmly pressed damp soil. A film of kitchen cellophane over the surface helps keep conditions moist and after a few days of temperatures around 20-25°C the seeds should germinate. Growing from cuttings of 'mother' plants is an alternative to growing from seeds.

In the first stages of life the seedlings are happy to start with lower light intensities often a meter below an HPS light or closer to fluorescent lights. The artificial lights are normally 'on' for 18-24 hours per day. During this time the seedlings are in a state of vegetative growth, they will continue to grow roots, leaves and branches but no bud.

By reducing daily light to ~12 hours the cannabis plant transitions into the 'flowering' phase. This stage normally requires 8-10 weeks (but more for certain strains) and it is during this time that the female flowers form. During this stage the plants gain a lot of bulk and will tolerate more nutrients and very bright light.Some growers introduce supplemental lighting to ensure the very best yields. At the end of this process, the plant is cut down and the buds (unpollinated female flowers) are dried. Some growers harvest the plants when they see the trichomes start to transition from clear to cloudy (this re□uires a powerful magnifying glass/scope to see). This often coincides with the bud producing lots of red/orange pistil hairs. Some smokers prefer bud harvested early, others prefer late-harvested bud. When growing your own, it is you that decides exactly how you like it!

In general, longer periods of vegetative growth will grow larger plants and support greater yields during subse□uent flowering. Typically

2-6 weeks of vegetative growth are used and during subse□uent flowering the plants may increase to 2 or 3 times their original height. Some growers use the 'sea of green' (SOG) method, this uses just a few days of vegetative growth before switching to 'flowering' conditions. This techni□ue produces small plants of low/medium yield, but allows for fast production.

Male plants are nearly always destroyed by the indoor grower as they don't yield any buds, and given the chance they will pollinate the female plants reducing them to seed.

Feminised seeds are popular with the indoor growers as they virtually eliminate the possibility of male plants. For many indoor growers feminized seeds from a □uality supplier are regarded as the only way to go. If male flowers appear at the end of a female flowering cycle don't panic, simply pinch off the male flowers. The female buds are mature and unaffected by the appearance of isolated rogue male flowers late in the flowering cycle.

The indoor grow room allows plants to be grew in soil or any number of other grow mediums. When growing in soil the cannabis plant benefits from 25% perlite or coco fibre being included. This allows better aeration of the soil. One common mistake by inexperienced growers is the tendency to overwater soil-grown plants. Get to know the weight of your plant pots and water only when the plants need it. Over watering, soil-grown plants will reduce yield/□uality and slow down plant development.

Growing cannabis indoors will require use and understanding of plant feeds. This is not complicated, all the plant feed does is deliver essential nutrients to the roots, it doesn't matter whether the roots are growing in clay pebbles, rockwool, coir or a hydroponic system. Even soil-grown plants will need additional nutrients when the soil has been depleted. Read the instructions on the nutrient labels and avoid the beginners temptation to exceed recommended levels. The experienced gardener can 'read' his plants and will learn when to water and feed plants.

Indoor growing allows the plants to develop under closely supervised grow conditions without the normal array of outdoor pests. Once the grower has the right system in place it is a predictable way of growing great quality cannabis, alot better than weed sold by street dealers. The main challenge for many indoor growers is dealing with the characteristic cannabis smell so that no-one notices it.

Recreational and medical cannabis popularity now extends far outside the earths warm/tropical climates, so for many growing cannabis indoors is the only option. Growing cannabis indoors has never been as popular as it is today, nor has it been as easy to produce superb quality weed. Professional seed suppliers, equipment providers, advice, and information are all available on the internet.

Of course,it all really begins with great quality seeds – get them from a supplier you can trust.

Medical marijuana- wonder drug or dangerous herb?

Marijuana is a known dangerous drug that is kept illegal alongside other dangerous substances like cocaine, PCP and heroin. To some people, it should remain that way, however, there are some who strongly insist that marijuana should be legalized. This is because they believe that this herb brings no danger to one's self or anyone. There are even groups of individuals pointing out the medical benefits of marijuana, which should not be denied to people. Still, there are some people who believe that marijuana should be further explored before making any actions.

As debates and arguments regarding medical cannabis continues to drag on, more and more researchers are continuing with their tests regarding the use of medical marijuana. Others have even come up with various strains of marijuana, which can help in treating certain illnesses. As more of these tests and researches provide scientific and credible results, more and more medical experts are seeing the potential of medical marijuana. In fact, many states today are supporting the use of it for medicinal purposes.

Indeed, every drug has a risk, including the most common ones that are found inside medicine cabinets. Medical experts and doctors would often balance the risks against the good these medicines would bring. It is now being done with cannabis as well. The truth is many researchers and experts have found out that marijuana has alot of medical benefits. It can provide relief to ailments that has symptoms of chronic pain like cancer and severe arthritis. Moreover, it is said to provide relief to AIDS wasting syndrome as well as the nausea during chemotherapy sessions.

Science has also proven the risks of marijuana, but these risks are outweighed by the benefits for the risks are very small. According to several research, medical marijuana's side-effects would be the euphoric mood swings, relaxed and/or impaired motor functions as well as increase in appetite. Compared to other medications that may provide the same results as medical marijuana, this herb doesn't have long-term side-effects and has no risks of overdose.

With all the good talk about medical cannabis, doctors would still say that the danger of using cannabis is not gone. The main concern they have is the effect of cannabis smoke. This smoke has more harmful chemicals and tar as compared to a regular cigarette. Though this is a proven thing, there's no way you can smoke 20 sticks of marijuana per day. Moreover, many gadgets have been introduced in the market today, which vaporizes marijuana instead of smoking it.

CHAPTER 5- CONCLUSION

Marijuana is one of the most abused drugs in the world. There is a ever-growing gap between the latest science about marijuana and the myths surrounding it. Some people think that since it is legal in some places, it must be safe. But your body doesn't know a legal drug from an illegal drug. It only knows the effect the drug creates once you have taken it. The purpose of this publication is to clear up some of the misunderstandings about pot.

Marijuana comes from the Indian hemp plant, and the part that contains the "drug" is found primarily in the flowers (commonly called the "buds") and much less in the seeds, leaves, and stems of the plant.

Marijuana, when sold, is a mixture of dried out leaves, stems, flowers and seeds of the hemp plant. It is usually green, brown or gray in color.

Hashish is tan, brown or black resin that is dried and pressed into bars, sticks or balls. When smoked, both marijuana and hashish give off a distinctive, sweet odor.

There are over 400 chemicals in marijuana and hashish.1 The chemical that causes intoxication or the "high" in users is called THC (short for tetrahydrocannabinol). THC creates the mind-altering effects that classifies marijuana as a "drug."

Plants, like animals, have traits that protect them in the wild. Plants can have colors or patterns that camouflage them from predators, or they can contain poisons or toxins that, when eaten, make animals sick or alter their mental capacity, putting them at risk in the wild. THC is the protective mechanism of the marijuana plant.

Intoxication literally means "to poison by taking a toxic substance into your body." Any substance that intoxicates causes changes in the body and the mind. It can create addiction or dependence, causing a person to want to take that drug even if it harms him or her.

You may have heard someone say that because marijuana is a plant, it's "natural" and so it's harmless. But it's not. Hemlock, a poisonous plant, is also "natural," but it can kill.

The other thing to know is that burning dried leaves and buds and inhaling the smoke into your lungs is definitely not "natural" and like smoking cigarettes, can be harmful to your body.

As for the medical uses of marijuana, it contains another chemical called CBD (short for cannabidiol). This is the substance most often associated with creating medical benefits. Unlike THC, CBD does not cause a high.2 Its medical benefits are still being studied, as are methods to breed marijuana plants with high CBD and low THC for medical use.

Marijuana is a drug like alcohol, cocaine, or ecstasy. And like these other drugs, it has side effects that can be harmful.

HOW IS IT USED?

Marijuana is a mixture of dried-out leaves, stems, flowers and seeds of the hemp plant. It is usually green, brown or gray in color.

Marijuana is a mixture of dried-out leaves, stems, flowers and seeds of the hemp plant. It is usually green, brown or gray in color.

Hashish is tan, brown or black resin that is dried and pressed into bars, sticks or balls. When smoked, both marijuana and hashish give off a distinctive, sweet odor.

Hashish is tan, brown or black resin that is dried and pressed into bars, sticks or balls. When smoked, both marijuana and hashish give off a distinctive, sweet odor.

Marijuana can be smoked as a cigarette (joint), but may also be smoked in a dry pipe or a water pipe known as a "bong." It can also be mixed with food and eaten or brewed as tea. These are called "edibles. Sometimes users open up cigars and remove the tobacco, replacing it with pot—called a "blunt." Joints and blunts are sometimes laced with other, more powerful drugs, such as crack cocaine or PCP (phencyclidine, a powerful hallucinogen).

When a person inhales the smoke from a joint or a pipe, he usually feels its effect within minutes. The immediate sensations—increased heart rate, lessened coordination and balance, and a "dreamy," unreal state of mind—peak within the first 30 minutes. These short term effects usually wear off in two to three hours, but they could last longer, depending on how much the user takes, the potency of THC and the presence of other drugs added into the mix.

Marijuana and Cancer - Governmental Arrogance Buries Viable Cancer Therapies

It seems that nearly everyone in government fancies himself superior to the rest of us in knowledge and judgment. There is no telling how much beneficial, not to mention vital, research and knowledge have been lost as a result of the arrogant whims of the few who consider themselves the elite among us, simply on the basis of having engineered themselves into a position of power. A depressing example of this arrogance is reflected in the fiasco surrounding research into the medical benefits of marijuana.

Way back in 1974, the National Institute of Health funded research at Medical College of Virginia. Their mission was to prove the contention that marijuana damages the immune system. In funding this research, the NIH was destined to be roundly disappointed - they effectively shot themselves in the foot. Rather than receiving confirmation and supporting evidence of their contention, the NIH people were annoyed to learn that the MCV researchers found instead, that THC, the active ingredient in cannabis, undeniably slowed the growth of three kinds of cancer in mice.

Since this failed miserably in bolstering the government's case against marijuana, in their view the most noxious of all weeds, and in fact proved just the opposite, the DEA came charging into the fray, banners flying, trumpets blaring. They shut down the Virginia study along with all other cannabis tumor research.

Not to be outdone in the public assault on a useful albeit often misused plant and substance, President Gerald Ford got on the bandwagon in 1976, and put an end to all cannabis research while simultaneously granting that right exclusively to the maniacally delighted pharmaceutical industry.

Then again, in 1983, in accommodation to intense lobbying and reception of massive campaign contributions, the Reagan/Bush administration tried hard to persuade American Universities and researchers to destroy all of the 1966-76 cannabis research work, including compendiums in libraries. They were partially successful. Large amounts of information have disappeared.

But all this negative effort is like trying to hold back the dawn. The facts keep cropping up in spite of the best efforts of vested interests to bury them. In February of 2000, another confirmation of marijuana's cancer-fighting abilities came out of Madrid. Researchers there had destroyed incurable brain cancer tumors in rats by injecting them with THC. This confirmed the earlier Virginia study.

The news of this discovery has been virtually non-existent in the United States. The New York Times ignored the story. So did the Washington Post and the Los Angeles Times. These papers receive major advertising revenues from the pharmaceutical industry, which by the way, employs two lobbyists for each and every member of congress.

As public pressure to allow the use of medicinal marijuana continues to build, more and more politicians are being induced to taking a closer look at the facts. Its strong support by patients and medical professionals is beginning to be felt. More and more states are adopting compassionate laws toward medicinal marijuana as many patients clamor for the substance to relieve the symptoms and side effects of chemo.

The nausea, vomiting, pain, and insomnia that are typically a conse☐uence of conventional cancer therapy, cripple a patient's ☐uality of life. Marijuana, smoked, vaporized, infused in teas, or baked in foods, can dramatically restore a patient's place in the world. Noting this has induced the entire oncology community to endorse its use.

The pharmaceutical companies, hard pressed to compete against this tidal wave of sentiment, have isolated the active compound in marijuana, delta-9-tetrahydrolcanabinol, THC, and made a synthetic version of it available by prescription. But it doesn't work nearly as well as plain old marijuana, it doesn't work at all on some people, it takes from 45 minutes to 2 hours to take effect when it does work, and it will set a patient back about $ 800.00 a month. Not really a good alternative.

Medicinal marijuana is not without its own side effects. Anxiety, drowsiness, dry mouth, slow reaction times, and loss of short term memory are among them. Patients using this substance for medicinal purposes will experience varying side effects. Everyone reacts differently to its use and it is very important to buy marijuana from an authorized source. Other drugs or harmful substances are often added by unscrupulous criminal dealers.

Doctors treating cancer patients are in critical need to be kept informed of all drugs taken by their patients, including marijuana, over-the-counter, prescription, or homeopathic remedies. It's very important to keep in mind that marijuana, at this point, is not a form of treatment and is not curative. It is used only to treat cancer symptoms like pain and to relieve the side effects of treatment.

Fourteen states have legalized the use of medicinal marijuana. They are Alaska, California, Colorado, Hawaii, Maine, Maryland, Michigan, Montana, Nevada, New Mexico, Oregon, Rhode Island, Vermont, and Washington. Each state has its own rules and regulations regarding its use and these need to be complied with. Most states require registration with supporting documentation and certification by a physician. This should by no means be construed as an endorsement for the indiscriminate use of marijuana. The substance has some very serious negative side effects and needs to be treated like any other drug. If you don't need it, stay away from it.

Made in the USA
San Bernardino, CA
24 December 2017